The Perky Little Pumpkin

A Halloween Story

By Margaret Friskey

Illustrated by Tom Dunnington

CHILDRENS PRESS®

CHICAGO

Library of Congress Cataloging-in-Publication Data

Friskey, Margaret, 1901-
    The perky little pumpkin : (a Halloween story) / by Margaret
Richards Friskey.
        p.   cm.
    Summary: A feisty little pumpkin achieves his goal of being
made into a jack-o-lantern at Halloween and seeks to scare the
costumed revelers around him.
    ISBN 0-516-03564-9
    1. Pumpkin—Fiction. 2. Jack-o-lanterns—Fiction.
3. Halloween—Fiction.] I. Title.
PZ7.F918Pep   1990   90-38376
[E]—dc20   CIP
                                            AC

Once upon a time
in a farmer's field
there were lots and lots
of pumpkins.

"Oh, my!" said the
biggest pumpkin. "I am
so big I will end up
in a pie, or be eaten
by a cow."

3

"Not me," said a perky
little pumpkin.
    "I am going to be
a jack-o'-lantern. I am
going to SCARE somebody."

A boy found the
little pumpkin and
made a jack-o'-lantern.

Now the perky
little pumpkin
had red glowing
eyes, a long nose,
and teeth sharp enough
to bite a bear.

The boy set the pumpkin
on a fence post.

His eyes glowed in
the dark. His nose was
long. His teeth were
sharp enough to bite
a bear.

He was all ready
to scare somebody.

It was very dark.
Thunder rumbled,
the wind whistled,
and the dry leaves
whispered, "Sh . . . sh."
An owl hooted far
away.
And there were strange
creatures all about.

Along came a pirate.
He laughed at the little
pumpkin on the post,
and gave him a poke
with his paper sword.

A witch flew by
on her broom.
    She did not even look
at the jack-o'-lantern.

A ghost rushed by
with just a sigh.
"Ooooo . . . oooo."

A ballerina danced
along, looking at the
sky.

"Shucks!" said the
jack-o'-lantern.
"I have not scared anyone
yet. But just you wait."

The wind howled.
Thunder rumbled.
Rain began to fall.
All the creatures fled
into the house.

Suddenly the little
pumpkin was snatched
from the post, and put
on a table in the hall.

The little pumpkin
looked up and saw
a fierce jack-o'-lantern.
It's eyes glowed red.
It's nose was long.
It's teeth were big
enough to bite a bear.

The little pumpkin
trembled.
Then he saw that the
fierce jack-o'-lantern
was shaking with fear.

"I did it!" cried the
little pumpkin.
I finally did it! I
scared somebody."
    He sighed a happy sigh
that blew his candle out.

About the Author

Margaret Friskey, Editor Emeritus of Childrens Press, was Editor-in-Chief of the company from its conception in 1945 until her retirement in 1971. It was under her editorial direction that Childrens Press expanded to become a major juvenile publishing house. Although she now has more free time, her days are by no means quiet. She spends time with her children, grandchildren, and great-grandchildren, many of whom live near enough to her little house in Evanston to visit often. She also has more time to concentrate on her writing.

About the Artist

Tom Dunnington hails from the Midwest, having lived in Minnesota, Iowa, Illinois, and Indiana. He attended the John Herron Institute of Art in Indianapolis and the American Academy of Art and the Chicago Art Institute in Chicago. He has been an art instructor and illustrator for many years. In addition to illustrating books, Mr. Dunnington is working on a series of paintings of endangered birds (produced as limited edition prints). His current residence is in Oak Park, Illinois, where he works as a free-lance illustrator and is active in church and community youth work.